Lost and Found:

The Adventures of

MARCO THE CAT

Austin J. Bell

Illustrated By Kayleigh Castle

the Peppertree Press
www.peppertreepublishing.com

MARCO THE CAT

For Chloe Evelyn Bell

For information regarding permission,
call 941-922-2662 or contact us at our website:
www.peppertreepublishing.com or write to:
the Peppertree Press, LLC.
Attention: Publisher
715 N. Washington Blvd., Suite B
Sarasota, Florida 34236

ISBN: 978-1-61493-859-0

Library of Congress Control Number: 2022918736

Printed October 2022

My name is Marco,
I'm a cat made of wood.

I look like a panther,
my artist thought I should.

5

I have lots of friends,

like Bird, Wolf, and Deer.

They're all different colors -
and what beautiful ears!

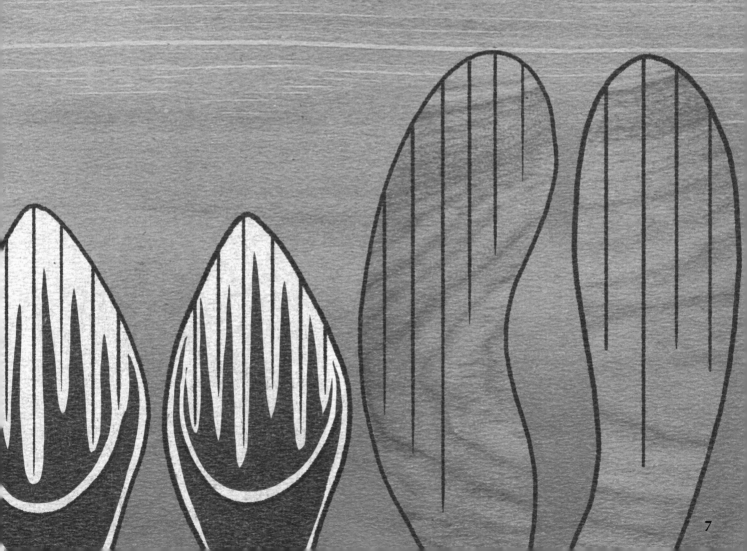

We lived on an island,
our place in the sun.

8

People danced all around us and had lots of fun.

One day a storm came
and washed us away.

Alone in the dark, I felt scared and afraid.

Where were my friends,
poor Bird, Wolf, and Deer?

They were lost in the mud,
no sign of them here!

One day a light shone down from the sky.

It was Florida sunshine,
    revealed by a guy!

The guy's name was Frank, he wa
from a museum.

He was happy to see me, some might say GLEESOME.

Before packing me up for a major ADVENTURE.

I traveled to Philly
and Washington too,

And posed behind glass,
JUST LIKE IN A ZOO.

I did this for years,
and enjoyed the attention,

But I missed
my friends, and
our home that I
mentioned.

Whatever happened to Bird, Wolf, and Deer?

I hadn't seen them for
one hundred years!

One day the museum sent me
on vacation, "Marco Island"
they called my new destination.

The place was familiar, with old sights, smells, and faces,

28

There were Bird, Wolf, and Deer, back home of all places!

We were happy to all be together again,

Though older and frailer,
we still were best friends.

Pelican Figurehead, Painted
Wood
Key Marco
A.D. 500–1500
Loaned by the Penn Museum

Wolf Figurehead, Painted
Wood
Key Marco
A.D. 500–1500
Loaned by the Penn Museum

Deer Figurehead, Painted
Wood
Key Marco
A.D. 500–1500
Loaned by the Penn Museum

Together we gathered in a museum
exhibit, to share our story with
others, if they'd believe it.

Bird, wolf, and deer figurehead likenesses reproduced by permission of the Penn Museum. Special thanks to artist Merald Clark for his contributions to this work.